how2become

KS2 SCIENCE IS EASY

BIOLOGY

THE
REVISION
SERIES

www.How2Become.com

As part of this product you have
also received **FREE** access to online
tests that will help you to pass
Key Stage 2 SCIENCE *(Biology)*.

To gain access, simply go to:

www.PsychometricTestsOnline.co.uk

Get more products
for passing any test at:

www.How2Become.com

Orders: Please contact How2Become Ltd, Suite 14, 50 Churchill Square Business Centre, Kings Hill, Kent ME19 4YU.

You can order through Amazon.co.uk under ISBN 978-1910602904, via the website www.How2Become.com or through Gardners.com.

ISBN: 978-1910602904

First published in 2016 by How2Become Ltd.

Typeset for How2Become Ltd by Anton Pshinka.

Disclaimer

CONTENTS

Evolution and Inheritance

THE
REVISION
SERIES

GUIDANCE
FOR PARENTS

Whilst the SATs are a daunting, disliked and often maligned concept, they remain an essential part of a child's education. Children should be provided with the best tools and guidance to enhance their intellectual ability and improve their performance.

The purpose of this section is to guide you through the KS2 Science (Biology) exam. It will allow you to familiarise yourself with all of the important information, advice and tips that your child will need in order to achieve SATs success.

The NEW SATs

From the summer of 2016, the SATs will undergo considerable changes, as dictated by the new national curriculum.

The purpose of the new and revised SATs is to ensure these tests remain rigorous, and therefore prove to be of a much higher standard compared to previous years.

With the new national curriculum comes a new marking scheme. Whilst we cannot provide details of exactly what this marking scheme consists of, we know that your child's tests will be marked externally. The scores of these tests will be used to monitor the progress of each school's performance, which is done via Ofsted reports and league tables.

Ultimately, your child's scores in their SATs will be used in conjunction with classroom assessments to provide a general overview of their attainment and progression during that academic year.

For more information on the new national curriculum, please visit the Department for Education section of the Government's website.

When Do the New SATs Come into Place?

The new national curriculum for Key Stage 2 SATs will be assessed for the first time in May 2016.

What do the New SATs Cover?

The national curriculum for Key Stage 2 SATs will consist of the following:

- English Reading (Comprehension)
- English Grammar (Grammar, Punctuation and Spelling)
- Maths (Arithmetic and Reasoning)
- Science (Biology, Chemistry, Physics)*

*(*Please note that not all children completing the SATs will sit a Science SAT. A selection of schools will be required to take part in a science sampling every other year.)*

For more revision guides including KS2 Science is Easy: Physics and KS2 Science is Easy: Chemistry, as well as KS2 Science is Easy: Practice Papers, please visit www.amazon.co.uk, and type the book title into Search.

Top Tips For Parents

In order for your child to score highly in their SATs, you need to ensure that they have everything they need to achieve high marks!

It is important that you and your child are fully aware of what the SATs consist of. The more familiar you are with what to expect, the better their chances will be when they sit down to take the tests.

Below is a list of GOLDEN NUGGETS that will help you AND your child to prepare for the Key Stage 2 SATs.

- ## Golden Nugget 1 – Revision timetables

When it comes to exams, preparation is key. That is why you need to sit down with your child and come up with an efficient and well-structured revision timetable.

It is important that you work with your child to assess their academic strengths and weaknesses, in order to carry out these revision sessions successfully.

TIP – Focus on their weaker areas first!

TIP – Create a weekly revision timetable to work through different subject areas.

TIP – Spend time revising with your child. Your child will benefit from your help and this is a great way for you to monitor their progress.

- ## Golden Nugget 2 – Understanding the best way your child learns

There are many different ways to revise when it comes to exams, and it all comes down to picking a way that your child will find most useful.

Below is a list of the common learning styles that you may want to try with your child:

- **Visual** – the use of pictures and images to remember information.
- **Aural** – the use of sound and music to remember information.
- **Verbal** – the use of words, in both speech and writing, to understand information.
- **Social** – working together in groups.
- **Solitary** – working and studying alone.

Popular revision techniques include: *mind mapping; flash cards; making notes; drawing flow charts* and *diagrams*. You could instruct your child on how to turn diagrams and pictures into words, and words into diagrams. Try as many different methods as possible to see which is most successful for your child's learning style.

> *TIP – Work out what kind of learner your child is. What method will they benefit from the most?*
>
> *TIP – Try a couple of different learning aids and see if you notice a change in your child's ability to understand what is being taught.*

• Golden Nugget 3 – Break times

Allow your child plenty of breaks when revising.

It's really important not to overwork your child, particularly for tests such as the SATs which are not marked on a pass or fail basis.

> *TIP – Practising for 10 to 15 minutes per day will improve your child's ability to engage with the topic and learn in a way that is simple yet effective.*

• Golden Nugget 4 – Practice, practice and more practice!

Purchase past practice papers. Although the curriculum will have changed for 2016, practice papers are still a fantastic way for you to gain an idea of how your child is likely to be tested.

- ## Golden Nugget 5 – Variety is key!

Make sure that your child reads a variety of different biology modules. This will be required if they wish to score high marks overall on their Science exam.

TIP – Spend some time with your child and write a list of all the key areas and topics that need to be covered. This way, your child will be able to tailor their revision to each module to ensure they know how to answer topical questions.

- ## Golden Nugget 6 – Encourage your child to discuss their work

When your child is undergoing practice questions, ask your child to talk about what they have just learnt. Did they understand it? Did they know what all the words meant?

TIP – Sit down with your child and ask them questions about what they have just read. Have them read a page and then test their knowledge by creating questions about the text. Have they understood everything?

- ## Golden Nugget 7 – Stay positive!

The most important piece of preparation advice we can give you is to make sure that your child is positive and relaxed about these tests.

Don't let the SATs worry you, and certainly don't let them worry your child.

TIP – Make sure the home environment is as comfortable and relaxed as possible for your child.

• Golden Nugget 8 – Answer the easier questions first

A good tip to teach your child is to answer all the questions they find easiest first. That way, they can swiftly work through the questions before attempting the questions they struggle with.

TIP – Get your child to undergo a practice paper. Tell them to fill in the answers that they find the easiest first. That way, you can spend time helping your child with the questions they find more difficult.

Spend some time working through the questions they find difficult and make sure that they know how to work out the answer.

THE
REVISION
SERIES

PLANTS

PLANTS

UNDERSTANDING PLANTS

In this chapter, we are going to talk about all things to do with plants, and look at what you will need to know when it comes to the Key Stage 2 assessments.

Not only is learning about how plants grow and survive extremely interesting, it is also very important; as plants make up a vital part of the world around us. As humans, we rely on them for food, materials and countless other things to get us through everyday life.

There are four main things about plants that you'll need to know. In this chapter, we will look at them all in great detail and make sure that you are as knowledgeable as possible about the plant world!

Superhero Lalita is going to teach you four main things about plants!

1. The parts of a plant and the jobs they do;

2. What a plant needs to live and grow;

3. What plants do with water and how they use it;

4. The lifecycle of a plant.

So, let's get into it, starting with section 1!

PLANTS

1. THE PARTS OF A PLANT AND THE JONS THEY DO

The flower has bright colours and nice smells to attract bees that will pollinate the plant. Seeds will later develop in the flower, as this is also where the ovules are found.

The plant also needs enough space and warmth – find out more on the next page!

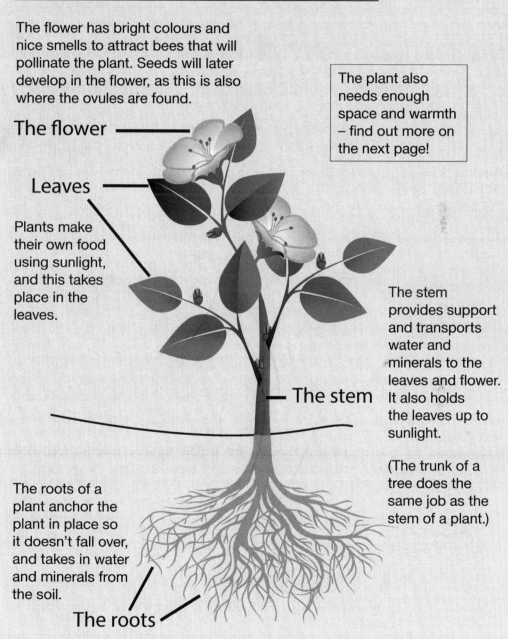

The flower

Leaves

Plants make their own food using sunlight, and this takes place in the leaves.

The stem provides support and transports water and minerals to the leaves and flower. It also holds the leaves up to sunlight.

The stem

(The trunk of a tree does the same job as the stem of a plant.)

The roots of a plant anchor the plant in place so it doesn't fall over, and takes in water and minerals from the soil.

The roots

PLANTS

2. WHAT A PLANT NEEDS TO LIVE AND GROW

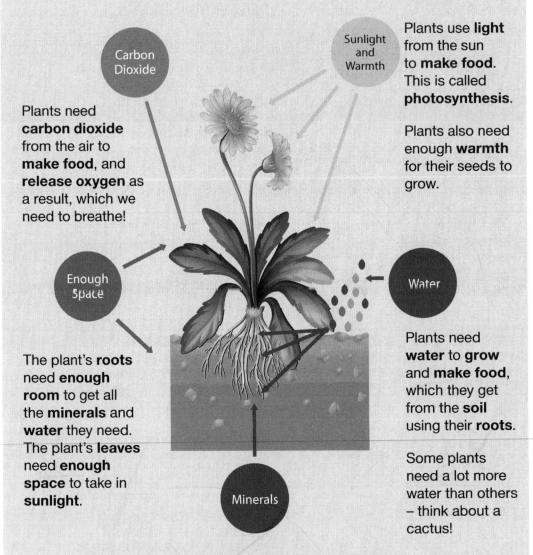

Carbon Dioxide

Sunlight and Warmth

Plants use **light** from the sun to **make food**. This is called **photosynthesis**.

Plants need **carbon dioxide** from the air to **make food**, and **release oxygen** as a result, which we need to breathe!

Plants also need enough **warmth** for their seeds to grow.

Enough Space

Water

The plant's **roots** need **enough room** to get all the **minerals** and **water** they need. The plant's **leaves** need **enough space** to take in **sunlight**.

Plants need **water** to **grow** and **make food**, which they get from the **soil** using their **roots**.

Some plants need a lot more water than others – think about a cactus!

Minerals

Plants take the **nutrients** they need through their **roots**, which are found in **minerals** in the **soil**.

3. WHAT PLANTS DO WITH WATER AND HOW THEY USE IT

Rain falls from clouds, giving soil moisture.

Finally, the leaves and flower receive the water they need.

Then, the stem sucks up the water from the roots.

First, the roots absorb water from the soil.

PLANTS

FUN EXPERIMENT!

Anil is doing an experiment. He wants to see how changing the amount of water a plant is given affects its growth.

He puts three pots filled with soil and a tomato seed on his windowsill, and gives each a different amount of water every day.

He recorded how high they grew in 1 month. Here are his results:

Tomato Plant	Location	Times watered per day	Height grown (cm)
1	Windowsill	1	6
2	Windowsill	2	11
3	Windowsill	3	15

To make sure he could reach a fair conclusion, Anil used the **same type of plant** in all three plant pots, and put them all on the windowsill, to ensure they received the **same amount of sunlight and air**.

This meant that the **only change** seen from plant to plant was the **different amounts of water** they received.

This is because he wanted to find out the **effect** that this **one thing** had on a plant's growth.

What is the conclusion we can make from Anil's experiment? How did increasing the amount of water affect the height that the plants grew?

4. THE LIFECYCLE OF A PLANT

THE FLOWER

On this page, we will look more closely at the parts of a flower, in preparation for learning about how plants reproduce.

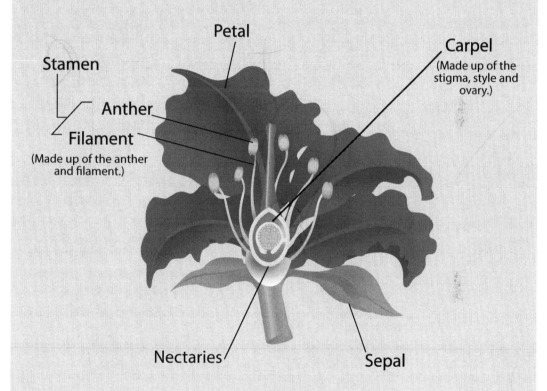

Petal

Carpel
(Made up of the stigma, style and ovary.)

Stamen

Anther

Filament

(Made up of the anther and filament.)

Nectaries

Sepal

The flower contains the plant's reproductive organs, and the ovules and pollen needed to create new seeds.

The pollen of one plant (found in the stamen) joins together with the ovules of another plant (found in the carpel), in order to form a seed.

Look on the next page to see what each part of the flower does!

PLANTS

WHAT EACH PART OF A FLOWER DOES

➤ **Stamens**

The stamen contains the pollen needed to fertilise an ovule (of a different plant) within the anther, which is held up by the filament.

➤ **Petals**

The petals are brightly coloured and smell nice in order to attract bees, who carry pollen from flower to flower.

➤ **Sepals**

Sepals are there to protect the flower bud in its early stages of life, and provide support for petals while they bloom.

Sepal

➤ **Carpel**

The carpel is made up of the ovary, the stigma and the style. The ovary contains the ovules, the stigma collects pollen from other plants, and the style supports the stigma, holding it up towards insects.

Bees land on or near the stigma to drink nectar, which is sticky to catch pollen.

Stigma

Style

Ovary

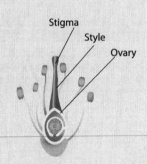

➤ **Nectaries**

The nectaries produce a sugary liquid called nectar, which plants use to attract insects. The nectar is almost like a reward for bees for carrying pollen from flower to flower.

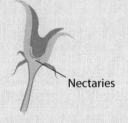

Nectaries

PLANTS

POLLINATION

So, we've looked at what the individual parts of the flowers do, but how do they work together to make seeds?

Pollen reaching the stigma of a plant = pollination

There are two main ways that pollination occurs:

THROUGH THE HELP OF INSECTS

1. When bees land on the flower to drink nectar, pollen from the stamens sticks to the bees' hairy legs. Then, when the bee goes to a different plant, this pollen sticks to the stigma, and reaches the ovule.

THROUGH THE HELP OF WIND

2. Some plants spread their pollen using the wind. These plants tend to have long filaments. This means that the anther is more exposed to the elements, and their pollen can be spread further.

PLANTS

FERTILISATION

Pollen joining with the ovule = fertilisation

So, when the pollen reaches the stigma of a plant, it travels down the style and into the ovary, where it can join with the ovules.

At this point, the ovules have been fertilised, and eventually become seeds.

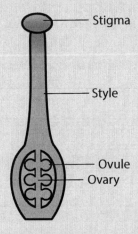

Next, the ovary – which is now full of seeds – will become a fruit, like an apple. Even dandelion seeds are technically classed as fruit!

This is called **sexual reproduction** – the male part of a plant (pollen) joins with the female part (ovule) of a different plant to produce new plants.

SEED DISPERSAL

Now the parent plant needs to spread its seeds as far as it can, to stop overcrowding. This reduces the amount of competition its seeds will face for space, light, water and nutrients.

This is why plants produce fruit – to spread their seeds!

Different fruits spread their seeds in different ways – there are 4 main methods of seed dispersal:

1. Using animals:

Tasty fruits are eaten by animals, and the seeds are swallowed. They travel long distances while in the animal's stomach, and then are excreted (pooed out) in a new location, where they can grow.

Alternatively, some fruits are sticky or clingy, and travel via animal fur.

Rabbit eats the seeds

Rabbit poos out seeds!

2. Using wind:

Plants like dandelions and sycamores have developed to be extremely good at using the wind, which helps them to fly huge distances away from their parent plant. The seeds have quite a slim chance of finding a suitable place to grow, which is why so many seeds come out when you blow on a dandelion – this gives them the best chance of producing new plants.

PLANTS

3. Using water:

Some plants that grow near seas and rivers have developed seeds that can float! The water can carry seeds huge distances, where they can find an ideal place to grow.

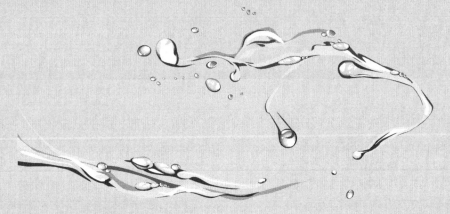

4. Using explosions:

This might be the most exciting thing a plant does to spread its seeds. Seeds that develop in pods (like peas) travel this way. When fully ripe, the pod dries itself up, which causes its skin to burst open, flinging out tightly-packed seeds in the process! This spreads the seeds out nicely to avoid overcrowding.

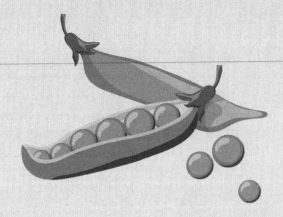

PLANTS

GERMINATION AND PLANT GROWTH

So, now that the seeds have been dispersed, how do they turn into plants?

Step 1:

If the seed is in an ideal location – one with enough **water**, **air** and **warmth**, then it will begin to **germinate** – green shoots will start to come out.

Step 2:

These shoots will then turn into a **seedling**; a young plant.

Step 3:

If the seedling has **everything it needs** to grow healthily (see page 18), it will develop into a **full-size plant**.

PLANTS

ASEXUAL REPRODUCTION IN PLANTS

Some plants can also use asexual reproduction to produce new plants. This means that sometimes, pollen, ovules and seeds are not needed to make new plants grow!

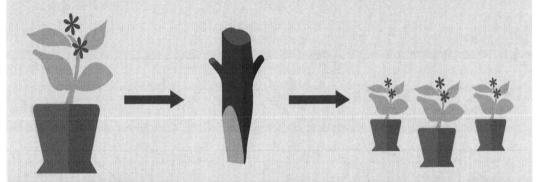

Some plants can grow from cuttings (small pieces) of other plants, without seeds!

If a cutting is in an ideal location, with soil and water, it can grow into a whole new plant of its own.

KEY POINTS:

- New plants are mostly made with two plants working together

- Less often, one plant can make new plants by itself – although this usually needs the help of humans

Question 1

Anil needs your help!

Label this diagram of a flower using the following choices:

Stem   **Roots**   **Leaves**   **Flower**

1 _____

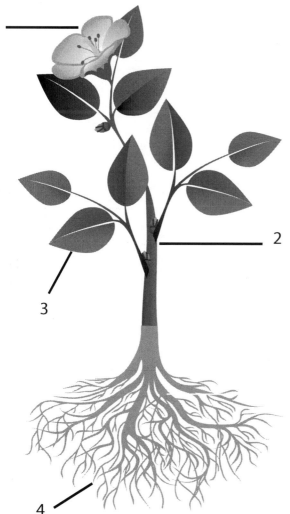

2 _____

3

4

1.

_____

2.

_____

3.

_____

4.

_____

Question 2

Identify these statements as being **TRUE** or **FALSE**:

a) The roots of a plant take in water from the soil. ＿＿＿＿＿＿

b) Pollen is made in a plant's leaves. ＿＿＿＿＿＿

c) Water travels through the stem to the leaves and flower. ＿＿＿＿＿

d) A plant's leaves only need sunlight to make food. ＿＿＿＿＿

For those you have answered **FALSE**, explain why you have made this choice.

＿＿＿＿＿＿＿＿＿＿＿＿＿＿＿＿＿＿＿＿＿＿＿＿＿＿＿＿＿＿＿＿＿＿＿＿＿

＿＿＿＿＿＿＿＿＿＿＿＿＿＿＿＿＿＿＿＿＿＿＿＿＿＿＿＿＿＿＿＿＿＿＿＿＿

＿＿＿＿＿＿＿＿＿＿＿＿＿＿＿＿＿＿＿＿＿＿＿＿＿＿＿＿＿＿＿＿＿＿＿＿＿

＿＿＿＿＿＿＿＿＿＿＿＿＿＿＿＿＿＿＿＿＿＿＿＿＿＿＿＿＿＿＿＿＿＿＿＿＿

Question 3

Name the 5 main things a plant needs to grow to its full potential.

1. ＿＿＿＿＿＿＿＿＿＿＿＿＿＿＿＿

2. ＿＿＿＿＿＿＿＿＿＿＿＿＿＿＿＿

3. ＿＿＿＿＿＿＿＿＿＿＿＿＿＿＿＿

4. ＿＿＿＿＿＿＿＿＿＿＿＿＿＿＿＿

5. ＿＿＿＿＿＿＿＿＿＿＿＿＿＿＿＿

Question 4

Anil and Freddie are having a conversation about plants and water.

Anil says:

"First, a plant's roots suck up water from the soil. Then, it travels up the stem, which carries it to the leaves and flower, where water is needed."

Freddie says:

"A plant's leaves catch rainwater, which travels to the rest of the plant from there. Roots are only there to hold it in place."

Who is right, and why?

_____

_____

_____

_____

Question 5

Anil wants to demonstrate how water is transported within plants. He knows that a good way to do this is with a white flower and some bright food colouring.

He knows all the steps for this test, but has forgotten the order in which he should do them in.

Help him out by putting the following jumbled-up steps in the correct order:

Add bright food colouring to the water

Cut a single stem and flower from a bunch

Wait a few hours – the petals will have changed colour!

Put the plant in the beaker

Fill a clear beaker with water

1. _____

2. _____

3. _____

4. _____

5. _____

Explain how this test demonstrates how water is transported in plants.

_____

_____

_____

_____

Question 6

On the left there is a diagram of a stamen (the male part of a plant). On the right is a diagram of a carpel (the female part of a plant).

Label each part of the diagram.

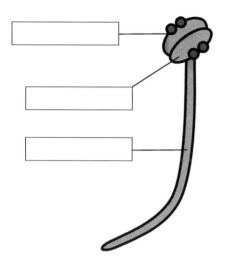
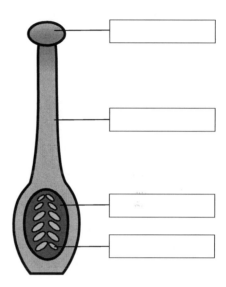

Question 7

Match the parts of the plant to their role, by drawing lines between the boxes. The first one has been done as an example.

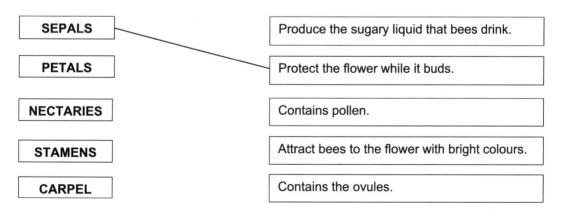

Question 8

From the following options, identify **three** things that flowering plants do to attract bees to their pollen.

Put a tick (✓) in the box next to the correct options, and a cross (✗) in the box next to the wrong option.

- Have brightly coloured petals which smell nice.

- Often have long stems.

- Dance about like bees themselves.

- Produce sugary nectar for them to drink.

Question 9

Anil and Lalita are discussing how some plants are pollinated by bees. Can you help them out? Complete the following sentences about pollination with one or two words, to let Anil and Lalita know what happens!

- When bees land on a flower, they touch the plant's ＿＿＿＿＿＿ , where the pollen is found.

- Bees are able to carry pollen because it sticks to their legs which are

  ＿＿＿＿＿ .

- When bees carry pollen and land on another flower, the plant's sticky ＿＿＿＿＿ catches it.

- This is called ＿＿＿＿＿ .

- Then, the pollen travels down the plant's ＿＿＿＿＿ , and into the plant's ＿＿＿＿＿ .

- Here, the pollen reaches the ＿＿＿＿＿ , and fertilises them.

- This causes them to develop into ＿＿＿＿＿ .

Question 10

Look at the following plants and decide whether you think they disperse their seeds using **animals**, **wind** or **explosions**. Give reasons for your answers, commenting on what the fruit is made of/its shape and size.

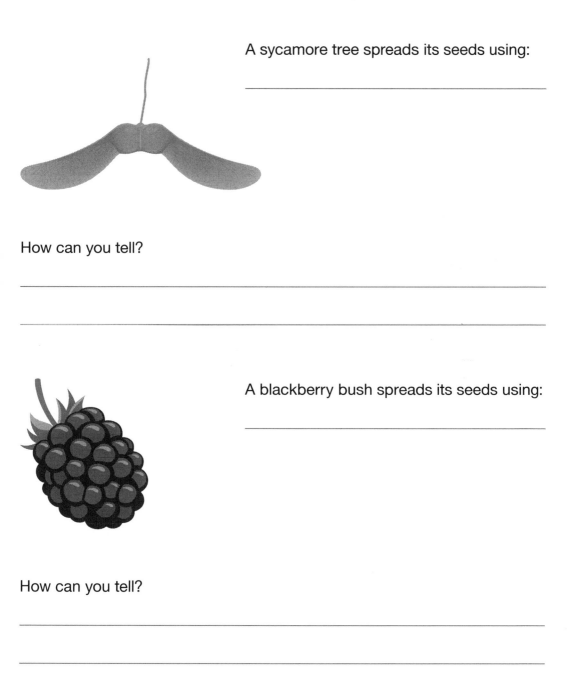

A sycamore tree spreads its seeds using:

_____

How can you tell?

_____

_____

A blackberry bush spreads its seeds using:

_____

How can you tell?

_____

_____

A violet flower spreads its seeds using:

_____

How can you tell?

_____

_____

ANSWERS TO PLANTS

Question 1

1. Flower
2. Stem
3. Leaves
4. Roots

Question 2

a) TRUE
b) FALSE
c) TRUE
d) FALSE

'b)' is false because pollen is made in a plant's flower, more specifically in the stamen's anther.

'd)' is false because a plant's leaves also need carbon dioxide, as well as sunlight, in order to make food.

Question 3

1. Sunlight / warmth
2. Carbon dioxide
3. Water
4. Enough space
5. Minerals

Question 4

Anil is right. Although he has not stated that soil gets water from rainfall, he has correctly described the way plants take in and transport water. Freddie, unfortunately, is completely wrong.

Question 5

1. Fill a clear beaker with water

2. Add bright food colouring to the water

3. Cut a single stem and flower from a bunch

4. Put the plant in the beaker

5. Wait a few hours – the petals will have changed colour

This demonstrates how water is transported in plants as it proves that a plant's stem can suck up water in order to move it to other areas of the plant. The fact that the dyed water was visible in the petals after it was only the stem that was put into it, demonstrates that the only way that a plant can get water to its leaves and flowers is via a stem or trunk.

Question 6

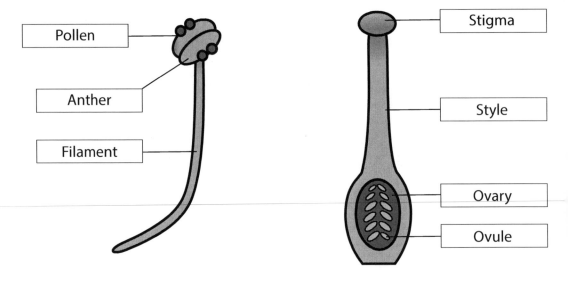

Question 7

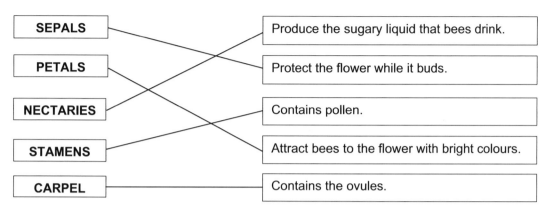

SEPALS	Produce the sugary liquid that bees drink.
PETALS	Protect the flower while it buds.
NECTARIES	Contains pollen.
STAMENS	Attract bees to the flower with bright colours.
CARPEL	Contains the ovules.

Question 8

- Have brightly coloured petals which smell nice. ✓
- Often have long stems. ✓
- Dance about like bees themselves. ✗
- Produce sugary nectar for them to drink. ✓

Question 9

- When bees land on a flower, they touch the plant's **stamen**, where the pollen is found.
- Bees are able to carry pollen because it sticks to their legs which are **hairy**.
- When bees carry pollen and land on another flower, the plant's sticky **stigma** catches it.
- This is called **pollination**.
- Then, the pollen travels down the plant's **style**, and into the plant's **ovary**.
- Here, the pollen reaches the **ovules**, and fertilises them.
- This causes them to develop into **seeds**.

Question 10

- A sycamore tree spreads its seed using **WIND**.

How can you tell?

The sycamore seed has light, aerodynamic wings that the wind can easily catch. It flies far from its tree with a helicopter-like motion.

- A blackberry bush spreads its seeds using **ANIMALS**.

How can you tell?

The blackberry bush produces a soft and juicy fruit – the blackberry – which provides many vitamins and minerals to animal carriers, who swallow its seed and spread it far from the parent bush. It is an appealing enough fruit that animals keep coming back for more!

- A violet flower spreads its seeds using **EXPLOSION**.

How can you tell?

The violet flower produces its seeds packed closely together in tight pods that point in three directions, so when the pod dries up and the seeds fly out, they do not all travel the same way reducing the amount of competition the seeds will face with each other for nutrients, water and sunlight. The seeds also develop to be an aerodynamic round shape for the best flight.

HOW ARE YOU GETTING ON?

THE
REVISION
SERIES

ANIMALS, INCLUDING HUMANS

ANIMALS, INCLUDING HUMANS

ANIMALS AND HUMANS

In this chapter, we will be discussing the bodies of animals and humans, and what they need to stay healthy and keep going. This includes their diets, and what their bodies do with food.

Also, we will look at the human body and how it develops from childhood to adulthood.

Our superhero Anil is going to teach you eight main things about animals and humans!

1. Nutrition

2. Food chains

3. Digestion

4. Skeletons, joints and muscles

5. Human organs

6. The circulatory system

7. Human development

8. Lifestyle and health

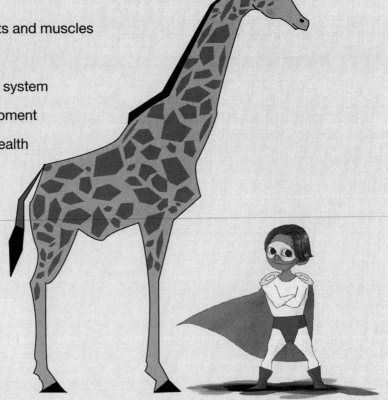

ANIMALS, INCLUDING HUMANS

1. NUTRITION

Unlike plants, animals (including humans) cannot produce their own food. So, we need to get our **nutrients** from food that we find in the world around us.

Of course, we need the right amount of certain types of nutrition in order to survive, grow and be healthy.

This pyramid shows the food groups needed for a balanced diet, as well as what the food supplies your body with (e.g. protein and fibre).

Look on the next page to see what these nutrients do for you!

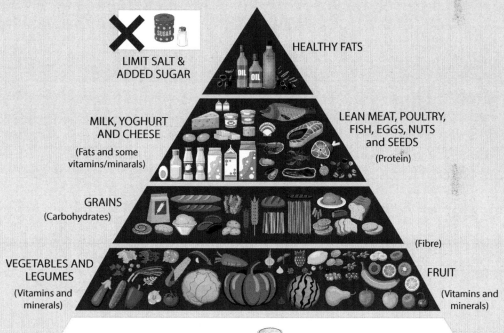

LIMIT SALT & ADDED SUGAR

HEALTHY FATS

MILK, YOGHURT AND CHEESE

(Fats and some vitamins/minarals)

LEAN MEAT, POULTRY, FISH, EGGS, NUTS and SEEDS

(Protein)

GRAINS
(Carbohydrates)

(Fibre)

VEGETABLES AND LEGUMES
(Vitamins and minerals)

FRUIT
(Vitamins and minerals)

DRINK WATER!

ANIMALS, INCLUDING HUMANS

Vitamins and Minerals: These provide the cells (which make up the body), with what they need to grow and survive – these are very important nutrients for any animal (including humans).

Fibre: Important for digestion.

Protein: This helps your body to grow and repair itself.

Carbohydrates: These either come in the form of starches (bread/pasta), or sugars (cake/biscuits) – both provide energy to your body, but too many can be unhealthy.

Fats: Small amounts of fats are important for giving you energy.

Can you name some examples of food/drink that would come under the following headings?

FIBRE:

_____

FAT:

_____

CARBS:

_____

PROTEIN:

_____

VITAMINS AND MINERALS:

_____

ANIMALS, INCLUDING HUMANS

2. FOOD CHAINS

Humans get most of their food from farmers, who sell it to shops so we can buy it. In the animal world, they have to be a bit more hands-on!

In nature, animals living in the same habitat depend on each other for food. We write down which animals eat what, by using a **food chain**.

Most food chains begin with **plants**, because they don't depend on anything but themselves to make their own food. Here is a common example of a food chain:

Grass produces its own food, then is eaten by rabbits, which are then eaten by foxes.

GRASS   RABBIT   FOX

The arrows point in the direction the energy and nutrients are travelling, they DON'T mean 'eats' – grass does not eat rabbits!

Within a food chain, the plant at the beginning of the food chain (e.g. grass/lettuce/flowers) is the **producer**, because it makes its own food.

All animals in the chain are **consumers**, as they depend on eating other things!

ANIMALS, INCLUDING HUMANS

In food chains, it is possible to identify animals which are killed and eaten (**the prey**), and the animals that do the killing (**the predators**). The producer (the plant) is neither.

Look at this food chain:

Plant leaf   **Caterpillar**   **Thrush**   **Hawk**

Can you work out which consumers are prey and which are predators?

Two of them are both!

Have a go at creating your own food chain, and work out what animals are the prey, and what animals are the predators.

ANIMALS, INCLUDING HUMANS

FOOD CHAINS VS. FOOD WEBS

Of course, food chains in nature are not always so simple!

When there are animals within a habitat that eat more than one thing, or are eaten by more than one thing, we can make a **food web**:

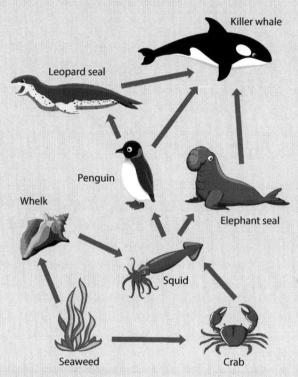

Things to look out for:

- Like a simple food chain, **it all begins with a producer**, which in this case is seaweed.

- The squid, for example, **preys on** more than one thing (whelks and crabs), and **is preyed on** by more than one thing (penguins and elephant seals).

- The killer whale has no predators, so this is **top of the food web**!

- You can look at this web and start to imagine what could happen **if something was removed** from it (see the next page for more on this).

ANIMALS, INCLUDING HUMANS

WHEN FOOD CHAINS GET INTERRUPTED

As we have learned, animals rely on each other for food in the wild. So, when species start to disappear or even become extinct, the lives of many other animals can be affected.

Look at this food chain and imagine this situation:

Grass   **Cricket**   **Toad**   **Snake**

In the area surrounding these animals' habitat, local farmers have increased the amount of pesticide they spread in their fields to combat the number of pests eating their crops.

This has resulted in the **number of crickets** in this area to **decline**, due to the chemicals in the pesticides.

Can you think of the effects this could have on **other** animal populations in this habitat?

Effects:

Reduced numbers of crickets means that the **toads have less food** to eat.

This causes the **number of toads in the area to decrease.**

Reduced numbers of toads means that the **snakes have less food to eat.**

This causes the **number of snakes in the area to decrease.**

Conclusion: The disappearance of just one species can hugely affect the entire ecosystem!

(Ecosystem = the community of living things in their environment and habitats.)

3. DIGESTION

So, we've looked at where animals (including humans) get their food, and therefore their nutrients. But how do their bodies actually absorb these nutrients?

In other words, what does the body do to food? What is extracted from these foods in order to keep the body functioning healthily?

Let's start by looking at the human digestive system:

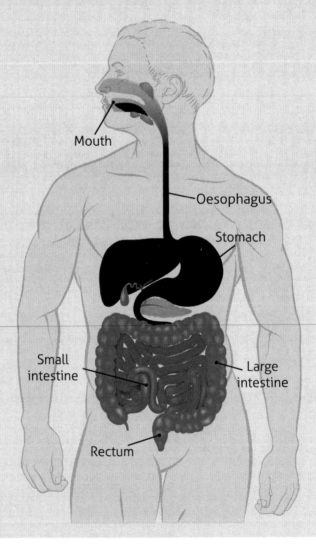

ANIMALS, INCLUDING HUMANS

STAGE 1

MOUTH AND TEETH

The first stage of the digestion process takes place inside the mouth. Food enters the body via the mouth, and is then chewed up and swallowed using the teeth and tongue.

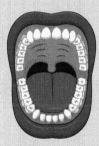

Humans have three types of teeth:

Incisors:

Your incisors are thin and flat to **cut food**.

Canines:

Humans only have four canines, which are sharp and pointy to **hold and tear food**.

Animal carnivores (meat-eaters) have prominent canines to kill and eat meat.

Molars:

Molars are the big teeth towards the back of your mouth.

They are large and wide in order to **crush and grind food up**.

ANIMALS, INCLUDING HUMANS

STAGE 2

OESOPHAGUS

After the food is swallowed, it travels down the oesophagus into the stomach. It's a human's food pipe.

STAGE 3

STOMACH

Your food will stay in your stomach for about four hours, while it gets broken down into smaller and smaller pieces by strong muscles and powerful juices.

STAGE 4

SMALL INTESTINE

Now that your food is in a 'liquidy' state, it travels to the small intestine where it is broken down even more. This is where the nutrients from your food are absorbed into your bloodstream!

STAGE 5

LARGE INTESTINE

Now, whatever's left (waste) passes into your large intestine. Here, water is absorbed, which means the remains of your food gets drier and drier until it becomes – you guessed it – poo!

STAGE 6

RECTUM

After the intestines have finished absorbing all that they can from your food, all that is left is waste. This waste (poo) eventually travels to the rectum, where it stays until it is pushed out through the anus. This happens when you go to the toilet!

4. SKELETONS, JOINTS AND MUSCLES

THE HUMAN SKELETON

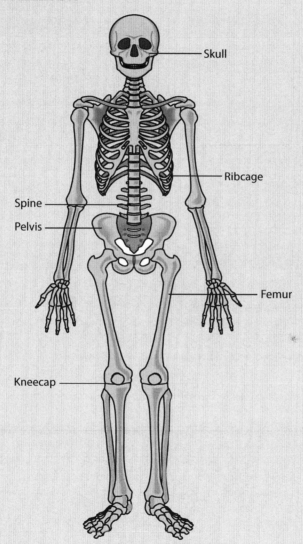

The skeleton plays three main roles in the body:

1. Supports your entire body.
2. Protects vulnerable areas of your body.
3. Allows your body to move! (See page 56.)

ANIMALS, INCLUDING HUMANS

➢ **SKULL**

The skull protects the organ that controls everything – the brain.

➢ **RIBCAGE**

The ribcage (made up of ribs) protects the heart and lungs. Humans have 24 ribs – 12 on each side.

➢ **SPINE**

The spine (backbone) protects the spinal nerve, which is vital for movement.

➢ **PELVIS**

The pelvis supports our spine and abdomen, as well as our legs. A woman's pelvis develops to be wider than a man's in preparation for having a baby.

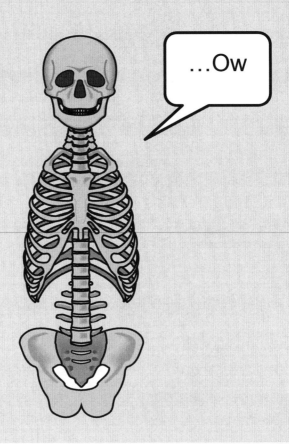

ANIMALS, INCLUDING HUMANS

SKELETONS OF THE ANIMAL KINGDOM

Most animals, including reptiles and fish, have a skeleton (like humans) formed of many bones to support and protect their bodies.

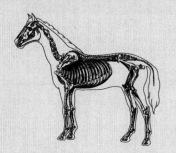

➢ **EXOSKELETONS**

Some animals have developed skeletons on the outside of their bodies. This includes species like crabs and lobsters, as well as many types of insect.

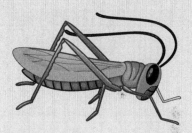

➢ **NO SKELETONS**

Some animals have developed no skeletal structure at all. Think of animals like worms and jellyfish – as well as snails that rely on shells! These are known as invertebrates (See more on page 87.)

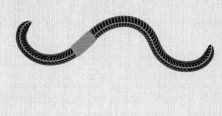

ANIMALS, INCLUDING HUMANS

JOINTS AND MUSCLES

While your skeleton gives your body shape and support, muscles and joints allow your body to move.

Your joints are found between many of your bones to join them together and enable you to flex and move. When your skeleton moves, your joints and muscles are put to work.

Joints are what join your muscles to your bones – they make it possible for the movement of your muscles to have an effect on your skeleton.

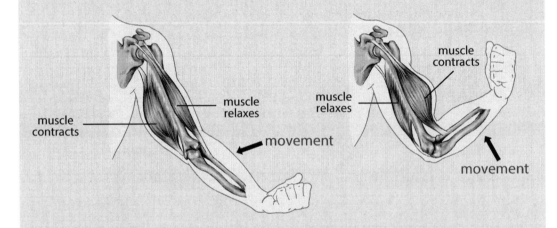

Muscles always work in pairs. While one muscle is active, it contracts, pulling the bone in one direction, while the corresponding muscle stays relaxed. For the opposite movement to be made, (e.g. to place your arms down by either side of your body), one muscle will contract, and the other will relax.

ANIMALS, INCLUDING HUMANS

5. HUMAN ORGANS

Your organs all do different jobs and are constantly working, even while you are asleep. While the brain controls all functions of the body, all of these organs listed below are vital for human survival, so it is very difficult to say which of the organs shown below is the most important.

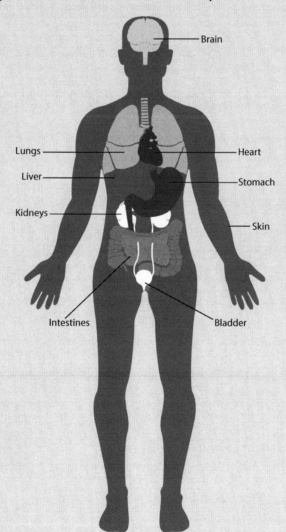

Now we've looked at where your organs are in your body, let's look at what they all do!

ANIMALS, INCLUDING HUMANS

➤ **BRAIN**

The brain is the body's control centre – it sends signals to the rest of your body. This makes your body parts do what they need to do. The brain is also responsible for thoughts, memories and emotions.

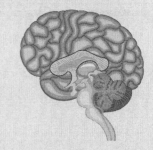

➤ **LUNGS**

The lungs are the squishy sacs where air goes when you breathe in. From this air, your lungs absorb vital oxygen, which they deliver to your bloodstream.

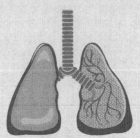

➤ **HEART**

The heart delivers blood, which carries oxygen and nutrients everywhere around your body. (See page 60 for more information!)

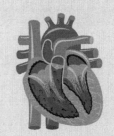

➤ **LIVER**

The liver does several extremely important things for your body. Firstly, it helps to clean your blood of toxins and absorb nutrients. It also produces bile, which is important for digesting fatty foods.

That's not all – the liver can even store and release extra energy for you if you get too tired!

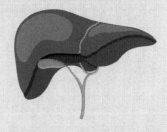

ANIMALS, INCLUDING HUMANS

➢ KIDNEYS

Your kidneys remove waste products and excess water from your bloodstream, and turns them into urine (wee). It also removes outside things that could be harmful to your body.

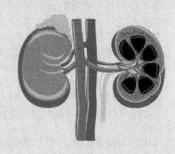

When blood enters the kidneys, the waste products are filtered out and sent to the bladder as urine.

➢ BLADDER

Your bladder is where the waste products from your bloodstream (urine) are stored by your body.

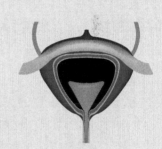

Urine collects here until it becomes too full, which is when you start to feel the uncomfortable sensation of needing the toilet!

➢ SKIN

Your skin is an organ, and the largest of all. It protects your body from outside harm, prevents things from leaking out of your body, and gives you a sense of touch.

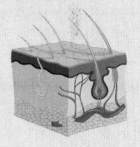

(For more on the stomach and intestines, see page 50.)

6. THE CIRCULATORY SYSTEM

The circulatory system is your body's way of transporting blood to everywhere that needs it.

The most important organ in the circulatory system is the **heart**, which pumps blood everywhere in your body. It is able to do this because it is basically one big muscle – it's incredibly powerful.

Blood travels within **arteries**, **veins** and **capillaries**:

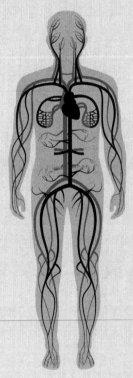

Arteries: The major vessels that carry blood away from the heart and towards the rest of your body.

Capillaries: Arteries branch out to become capillaries (smaller vessels), which supply blood to specific areas of the body.

Veins: The vessels that carry blood back to your heart, once your body has used the oxygen and nutrients from it.

ANIMALS, INCLUDING HUMANS

7. HUMAN DEVELOPMENT

Puberty – The development from childhood to adulthood that humans go through, approximately between the ages of 10-18.

During puberty, girls' bodies and boys' bodies change dramatically. Some changes happen to girls AND boys, some ONLY happen to girls, and some ONLY happen to boys. See below for the breakdown:

<u>Boys' and girls' bodies</u>

- Adolescents of both genders will grow in height;

- Body hair will start to grow;

- Bodies will start to sweat more;

- Acne (spots) will likely start to emerge.

<u>Just girls' bodies</u>

- Breasts begin to develop;

- Girls will begin to have their first periods – ovaries start to release eggs into the womb.

<u>Just boys' bodies</u>

- Testicles begin to produce sperm;

- Boys' voices become much deeper (girls' voices also become lower, but not as much as boys).

ANIMALS, INCLUDING HUMANS

8. LIFESTYLE AND HEALTH

As well as diet, there are many other aspects of life that can affect your health, including exercise (improving your health), and smoking (harming your health). Choices we make every day can be really beneficial to our body functions, or they can pose risks.

It is a good idea to be aware about how things can affect your body:

1. Exercise:

Exercising every day maintains good circulation, healthy lungs and strong muscles. It also keeps your brain sharp, and improves happiness.

2. Alcohol:

Drinking too much alcohol will damage your liver, as this is where your body processes it. Alcohol can also lead to problems with other organs, such as the brain and stomach. Alcohol can be addictive.

3. Smoking:

Cigarettes will damage your lungs – leading to cancer in serious cases. Cigarettes can be addictive.

4. Drugs:

'Drugs' is a very broad term most often used to describe consumable things containing chemicals which affect your body. For example, doctors use drugs to treat diseases.

Some drugs can cause harm to our bodies if misused, which is why many forms of drugs are illegal. These types of drugs can be addictive.

Question 1

Answer the following questions about diet:

a) Why do animals (including humans) need food?

_____

_____

_____

b) Why is it important to have a balanced diet?

_____

_____

_____

c) What should you not have too much of in your diet?

_____

_____

_____

d) What types of food should you eat the most of in your diet?

_____

_____

_____

Question 2

Look at the following list. Write **TRUE** if you think Anil's statement is correct, and **FALSE** if you think it is incorrect.

a) "Fruit and vegetables are a good source of vitamins and minerals."

Is Anil's statement true or false?

_____

b) "People should make an effort to add salt to their diet."

Is Anil's statement true or false?

_____

c) "Some foods can contain fat and minerals."

Is Anil's statement true or false?

_____

d) "Eating foods that are high in fibre will help you digest food."

Is Anil's statement true or false?

_____

e) "Protein is bad for you."

Is Anil's statement true or false?

_____

Question 3

Look at this food chain:

a) What does the mouse eat?

_____

b) What is the producer of this food chain? What does "producer" mean?

_____

_____

c) The mouse is the owl's prey. So, how can we describe the owl?

_____

d) Which is the only part of this food chain that is not a consumer?

_____

Question 4

Look at this food web:

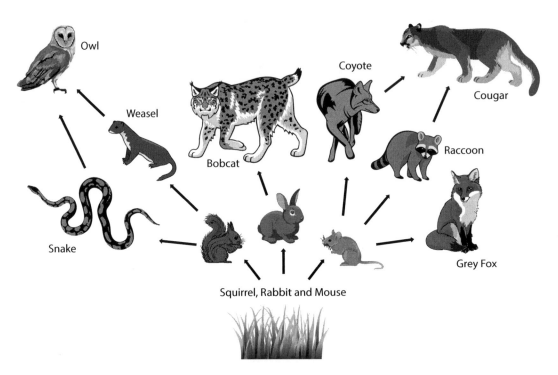

1. Write down three animals that are at the top of their food chains. What does this mean?

    _____

    _____

2. Think about what may happen to the population of weasels if the number of squirrels, rabbits and mice decreased. Write down your thoughts.

    _____

    _____

3. What would happen to the population of weasels if the number of owls decreased? Why?

_____

_____

_____

4. Which are the only three animals that are not predators?

_____

_____

Question 5

Look at this picture of a mouth. In the correct boxes, write down the types of tooth the lines are pointing to, using the list at the bottom of the page to guide you.

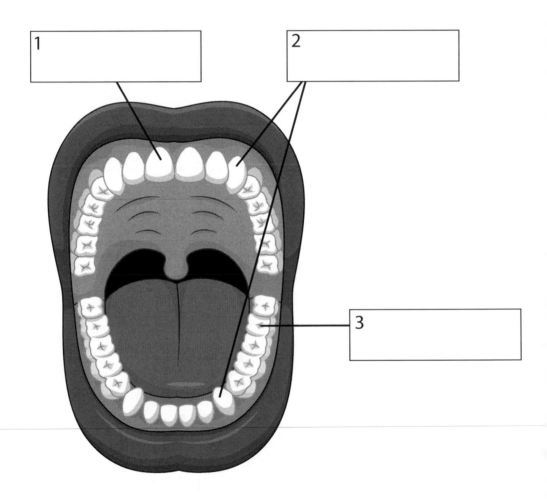

1. Teeth with a flat edge – used to cut food.

2. Teeth with a sharp edge – used to tear food.

3. Teeth that have a big and wide edge – used to grind food.

Question 6

Anil needs your help! Draw a line to match each body part to its role in the digestion system. <u>The first one has been done as an example.</u>

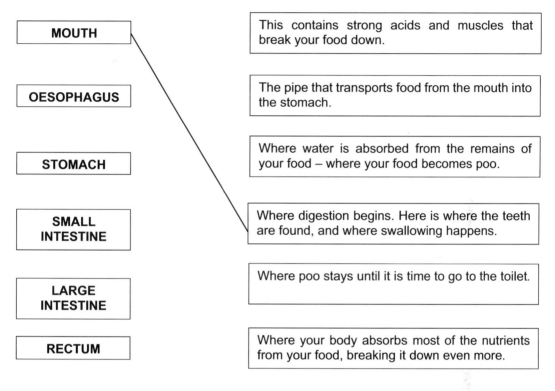

Body Part	Role
MOUTH	This contains strong acids and muscles that break your food down.
OESOPHAGUS	The pipe that transports food from the mouth into the stomach.
STOMACH	Where water is absorbed from the remains of your food – where your food becomes poo.
SMALL INTESTINE	Where digestion begins. Here is where the teeth are found, and where swallowing happens.
LARGE INTESTINE	Where poo stays until it is time to go to the toilet.
RECTUM	Where your body absorbs most of the nutrients from your food, breaking it down even more.

Question 7

These parts of a skeleton are arguing about who has the most important job to do in the human body, but they have left some gaps!

Fill in the blank spaces below:

> I'm the skull, so I'm clearly the best. My job is to protect the _____, the most important organ of all.

> That's all well and good, but I'm the ribcage. Within my 24 bones, you find the _____ – the organ that pumps blood around the whole body.

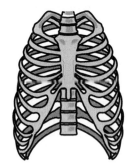

> I'm definitely the most important. As the spine, I hold the whole body up. Also, nothing would work without the _____, which I protect.

Which body part, if any, do you agree with? Why?

_____

_____

_____

_____

_____

Question 8

In the box are the names of 12 animals and insects. Below the box is a table with three columns, titled 'Skeleton', 'Exoskeleton' and 'No Skeleton'. Help Anil sort the animals into the correct columns!

Dog

Horse

Goldfish

Worm

Jellyfish

Crab

Spider

Lobster

Dolphin

Slug

Octopus

Locust

SKELETON	EXOSKELETON	NO SKELETON

Question 9

Look at the diagrams below, and label each box as 'contracted muscle' or 'relaxed muscle' based on the direction of movement (shown by the arrow).

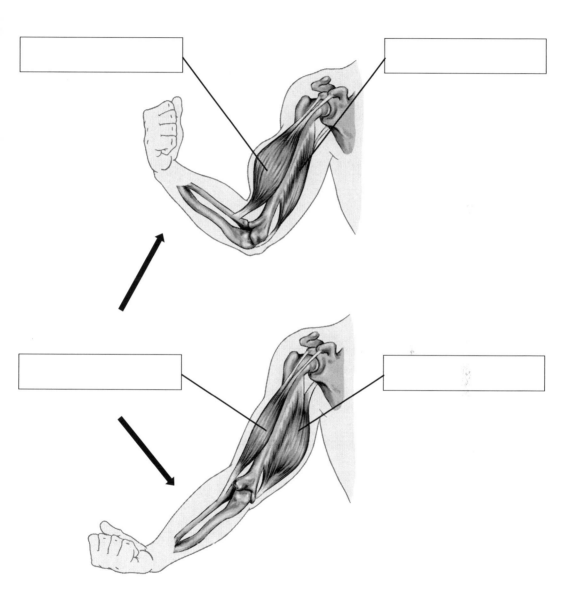

Question 10

Below is a list of definitions for organs of the human body. Match each one to the pictures of these organs by writing a number (1-7) in the given boxes. Also, write down the name of each organ on the line next to the pictures.

1. Absorb oxygen for the blood.

2. Where urine is stored.

3. Provides protection for the body and allows it to feel things outside the body.

4. Controls all processes of the body.

5. Turn waste into urine.

6. Pumps blood around the whole body.

7. A large organ that does many jobs, like removing toxins from the blood.

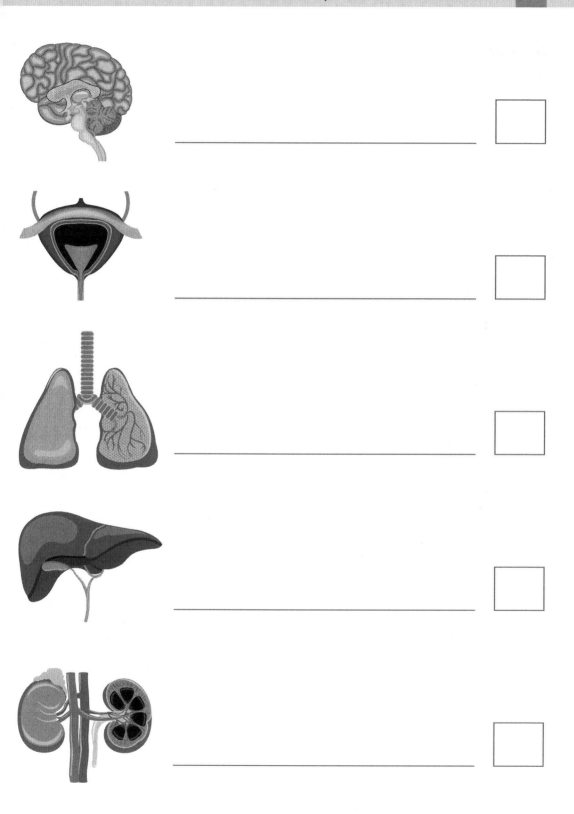

Question 11

Scarlett needs your help! She has written a report about the circulatory system, but has left some gaps. Fill them in for her.

The circulatory system refers to the way that _____ is transported around the bodies of humans and many other species of animal. It is controlled by the _____, which for humans beats around 70 times a minute.

Blood carries oxygen and nutrients that all body parts need to function. Firstly, the heart sends blood that is rich in _____ around the body, and the body uses this oxygen. The now deoxygenated blood then returns to the heart to replenish. The heart is able to re-oxygenate blood by using oxygen that comes directly from the _____. The process then starts again; it is a constant cycle.

There are three main types of blood vessel that transport blood to and from the heart. The major vessels that carry blood from the heart and to the rest of your body are called _____. These then split into _____ to deliver blood to specific areas of your body. The vessels that transport the deoxygenated blood back to the heart are called _____.

Question 12

1. What is puberty?

_____

_____

2. Name a change that happens to the bodies of boys and girls during puberty:

_____

3. Name a change that only happens to girls' bodies during puberty:

_____

4. Name a change that only happens to boys' bodies during puberty:

_____

ANSWERS TO ANIMALS, INCLUDING HUMANS

Question 1

a) Animals and humans need to eat in order to get nutrients like vitamins and minerals, protein, and fibre into their bodies. Their bodies need these nutrients to keep their organs working, repair their bodies, and move. Unlike plants, their bodies cannot produce food themselves, so they need to find food in the world around them.

b) It is important to have a balanced diet to make sure the body gets enough of all the types of nutrients it needs to be healthy, and not too much of potentially unhealthy things like fats and sugars.

c) You should not have too much of anything in your diet, but especially not things like fat, sugar, salt, or carbohydrates.

d) You should eat foods high in vitamins and minerals the most, as these are the most beneficial nutrients for your body. These are found mostly in vegetables, as well as fruit.

Question 2

a) **TRUE**

b) **FALSE** (salt is found in many foods and your body only needs very little of it)

c) **TRUE**

d) **TRUE**

e) **FALSE** (protein is vital for keeping muscles healthy – but it is possible to eat too much)

Question 3

a) The mouse eats the sweetcorn.

b) The producer of this food chain is the sweetcorn. This means that it does not rely on anything else to produce its food, and is the start of the food chain.

c) The owl can be described as a predator.

d) The only part of this food chain that is not a consumer is the sweetcorn.

Question 4

1. Your answers could be out of the following: the owl, bobcat, cougar and grey fox. These are all at the top of their food chains. This means that nothing eats them – they are predators only, never prey.

2. The rabbits, squirrels and mice are the weasel's food so if their numbers went down, some weasels would probably start to die out due to a lack of food.

3. Owls eat weasels, so if the number of owls went down, then the population of weasels would probably increase, as there would be fewer predators killing and eating them.

4. The rabbits, squirrels and mice are the only animals that are not predators, because they do not hunt for their food (grass). They are prey only.

Question 5

1. Incisor

2. Canine

3. Molar

Question 6

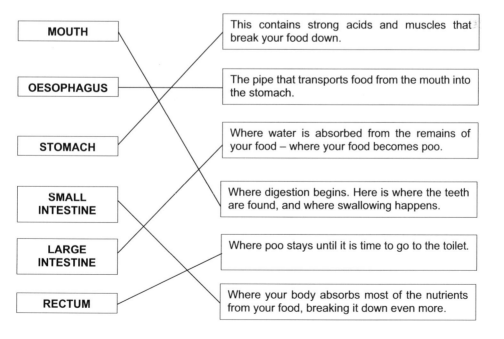

MOUTH	This contains strong acids and muscles that break your food down.
OESOPHAGUS	The pipe that transports food from the mouth into the stomach.
STOMACH	Where water is absorbed from the remains of your food – where your food becomes poo.
SMALL INTESTINE	Where digestion begins. Here is where the teeth are found, and where swallowing happens.
LARGE INTESTINE	Where poo stays until it is time to go to the toilet.
RECTUM	Where your body absorbs most of the nutrients from your food, breaking it down even more.

Question 7

I'm the skull, so I'm clearly the best. My job is to protect the **brain**, the most important organ of all.

That's all well and good, but I'm the ribcage. Within my 24 bones, you find the **heart** – the organ that pumps blood around the whole body.

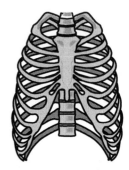

I'm definitely the most important. As the spine, I hold the whole body up. Also, nothing would work without the **spinal nerve**, which I protect.

(Your answer for the question: 'Which body part do you agree with?' can be any of the three if you've argued your point well – although all three are needed for humans to survive. Get a parent or teacher to check your answer!)

Question 8

SKELETON	EXOSKELETON	NO SKELETON
Dog	Crab	Jellyfish
Horse	Lobster	Worm
Goldfish	Locust	Slug
Dolphin	Spider	Octopus

Question 9

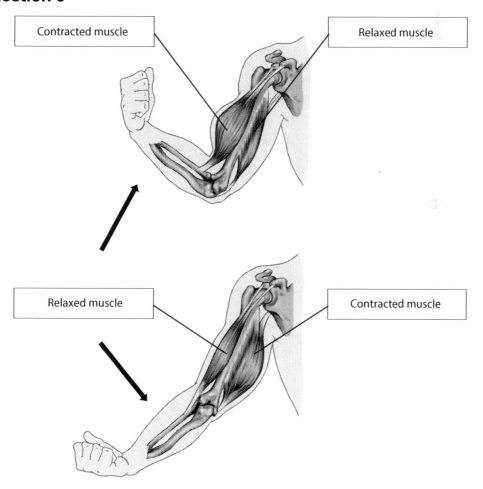

Question 10

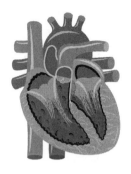

Heart 6

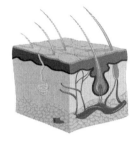

Skin 3

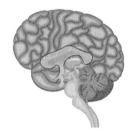

Brain 4

Bladder 2

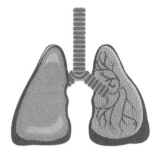

<u>Lungs</u>

1

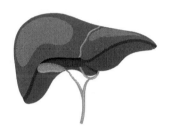

<u>Liver</u>

7

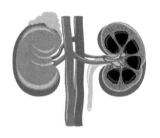

<u>Kidneys</u>

5

Question 11

The circulatory system refers to the way that **blood** *is transported around the bodies of humans and many other species of animal. It is controlled by the* **heart**, *which for humans beats around 70 times a minute.*

Blood carries oxygen and nutrients that all body parts need to function. Firstly, the heart sends blood that is rich in **oxygen** *around the body, and the body uses this* oxygen. *The now deoxygenated blood then returns to the heart to replenish. The heart is able to re-oxygenate blood by using oxygen that comes directly from the* **lungs**. *The process then starts again; it is a constant cycle.*

There are three main types of blood vessel that transport blood to and from the heart. The major vessels that carry blood from the heart and to the rest of your body are called **arteries**. *These then split into* **capillaries** *to deliver blood to specific areas of your body. The vessels that transport the deoxygenated blood back to the heart are called* **veins**.

Question 12

1. Puberty is the process that humans go through in the development from childhood to adulthood. Adolescents' bodies go through many drastic changes as they mature; girls' bodies and boys' bodies develop differently, although some changes happen to everyone.

2. Both boys and girls grow in height/grow body hair/start to sweat more.

3. Only girls develop breasts capable of feeding infants. Also, only girl's bodies start releasing eggs into the womb (periods start).

4. Only boys begin to develop sperm in their testicles. Boys also have a much more significant change in voice – it becomes much deeper.

HOW ARE YOU GETTING ON?

THE
REVISION
SERIES

LIVING THINGS AND THEIR HABITATS

LIVING THINGS AND THEIR HABITATS

1. GROUPING AND CLASSIFYING LIVING THINGS

As you can tell, certain types of living things have more in common with each other than other living things. You can look at these similarities and differences and group things together based on what you see.

For example, even recognising something as being an animal or a plant is using scientific classification! Below are the three main groups of how living things can be categorised.

Plants	Animals	Microorganisms
- Its roots are firmly embedded in earth. - Able to produce their own food.	- Able to move around. - Need to find food from outside sources.	- Humans cannot see them with their naked eye because they are too small – a microscope is needed. (*Micro* means 'tiny', and *organism* means 'living thing'.)

Also, it is possible to group living things together within these groups: they can have simple names of their own.

Again, this can be done in very general terms, or it can be quite specific.

See the next page for more!

INVERTEBRATES AND VERTEBRATES

Let's look at some ways you can group **animals** together.

For example, you can do this based on whether they have a skeleton or not. The name given to animals that have a skeleton is **vertebrate**. The name given to animals that don't have a skeleton is **invertebrate**.

Vertebrates – have a spine	**Invertebrates** – don't have a spine

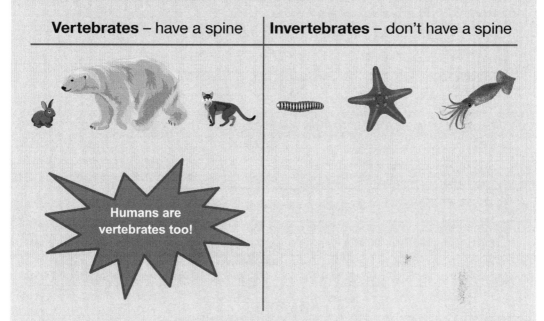

Humans are vertebrates too!

So, as you can see, grouping and classifying living things is done by looking carefully at what features and characteristics they have, and recognising when two or more living things share these features.

LIVING THINGS AND THEIR HABITATS

GROUPING VERTEBRATES

Have you heard the terms **mammal**, **amphibian** and **reptile**?

These are all words that are used to classify and group vertebrates based on their features and characteristics. Words like **fish** and **bird** are also used to classify animals.

Let's look at them more closely:

MAMMALS

- Mothers give birth to live babies, and produce milk to feed them;
- Have lungs to breathe air;
- Grow at least some hair or fur – many mammals' bodies are covered in fur;
- Are warm-blooded.

AMPHIBIANS

- Mothers lay eggs, usually in water;
- They hatch looking fishlike (tadpoles) with gills to breathe underwater;
- They later develop lungs so they can breathe air on land;
- Have slimy skin;
- Are cold-blooded.

LIVING THINGS AND THEIR HABITATS

MAMMALS

- Mothers lay hard-shelled eggs on land;
- Have lungs to breathe air;
- Have dry, scaly skin;
- Are cold-blooded.

BIRDS

- Mothers lay eggs;
- Have lungs to breathe air;
- Their bodies are covered in feathers to enable flight and keep them warm;
- Are warm-blooded.

FISH

- Mothers lay eggs;
- Have gills to breathe underwater – they cannot survive on land;
- Their bodies are covered in slimy scales to protect them and help them swim;
- Are cold-blooded.

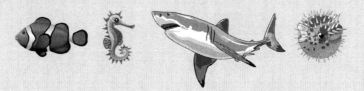

LIVING THINGS AND THEIR HABITATS

GROUPING INVERTEBRATES

So, we've looked at ways of classifying vertebrates. Now, let's look at ways of further classifying **invertebrates**.

INSECTS

-   Bodies are made up of three segments (one 'head' and two 'body' sections);
-   Have six legs;
-   Have two antennae;
-   Many have two wings;
-   Herbivores (eat plants).

ARACHNIDS

-   Bodies are made up of two segments ('head' and 'body');
-   Have eight legs;
-   Do not have antennae or wings;
-   Most are carnivores (eat other animals).

JELLYFISH

-   Bodies are 90% water – many are see-through;
-   Have tentacles which sometimes can sting;
-   Do not have brains;
-   Eat plants, plankton and small fish.

LIVING THINGS AND THEIR HABITATS

WORMS

- Bodies are long and tube-like;
- Most move using hairs to grip into the earth;
- Have a brain;
- Eat bacteria.

MOLLUSCS

- Bodies are soft and only consist of one part;
- Some have one foot (land-based molluscs);
- Some have tentacles (water-based molluscs);
- Some have shells.

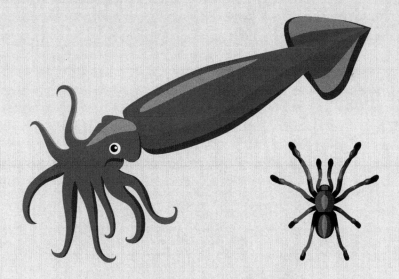

LIVING THINGS AND THEIR HABITATS

GROUPING PLANTS

Plants can be classified into two main groups: **flowering** and **non-flowering.**

Most plants that you see around you are **flowering** plants, even grass. Many trees also come under this category. Think of trees that lose their leaves in winter (**deciduous** trees). If it produces seeds (like acorns), it is a flowering plant.

Non-flowering plants refer to things like algae, seaweed, moss and ferns. Trees that do not lose their leaves in winter (**coniferous** trees) are also classed as non-flowering, as they produce cones, not seeds. Think of a pine tree that gives pine cones – this is a non-flowering plant.

LIVING THINGS AND THEIR HABITATS

CLASSIFICATION KEYS

Classification keys are a way to put living things into groups (e.g. **mammal**, **reptile** or **amphibian**), by asking a series of questions (usually **YES/NO**) about the appearance and features of that animal.

Keys are a great way of classifying an animal or plant if you aren't sure about what it is called or which group it should belong to.

Use the following key to sort these animals into groups, by testing each of them with the questions in the key:

| Badger | Lizard | Frog | Starling | Clownfish |

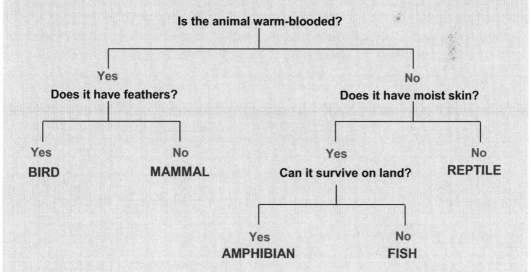

LIVING THINGS AND THEIR HABITATS

Keys can also be used to distinguish specific animals from each other. Look at this one about invertebrates, and identify what animals *a-e* are, by testing each one with the questions in the key:

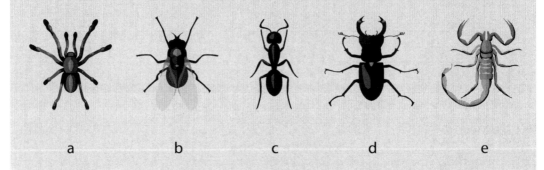

a   b   c   d   e

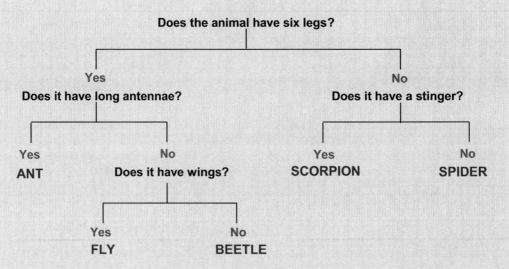

Does the animal have six legs?

Yes   No
Does it have long antennae?   Does it have a stinger?

Yes   No   Yes   No
ANT   Does it have wings?   SCORPION   SPIDER

Yes   No
FLY   BEETLE

LIVING THINGS AND THEIR HABITATS

2. ENVIRONMENTS AND HUMAN IMPACT

Where an animal lives is called its **habitat**. Of course, animals rely on their habitats for food and shelter. **The environment** controls how much food and shelter is available in these habitats: think about weather, temperature, and even disease.

As humans, the actions we take both individually and collectively can have a huge effect on the environment around us. So, they can have a huge effect on the habitats, and therefore the lives, of many species of animal that live both near and far away from us.

Examples:

1. Humans cut down trees to build houses. This causes animals that live in trees or get food from trees to die.

2. Humans throw litter into a pond which pollutes the water, making it harmful to animals that live there.

3. Humans build factories that pump fumes into the atmosphere. This causes nearby plants to die because they are not getting enough oxygen. This causes insects to die because they are not getting enough food. Anything that eats insects will now also have less food.

LIVING THINGS AND THEIR HABITATS

PROTECTING OUR ENVIRONMENT

Things like nature reserves and national parks exist in order to protect the habitats and animals in certain areas, and to ensure that species do not become extinct (die out). They provide a protected habitat where it is illegal to chop things down or build things.

LIVING THINGS AND THEIR HABITATS

3. LIFECYCLES AND REPRODUCTION

HUMAN LIFECYCLE

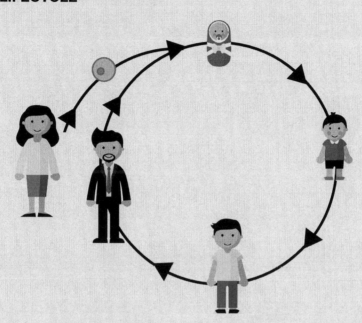

1. Human life begins when a sperm cell (from the father) joins with an egg cell (from the mother). The fertilised egg slowly becomes a baby during pregnancy, who is then born when he or she has developed enough – after about 9 months.

2. The baby will then become a child – still needing to grow and develop much more but will probably have learned to walk and talk. At this stage the child will have a set of milk teeth, which will be replaced by permanent 'adult teeth' by the age of about 13.

3. At around 10 years old, girls will start to begin puberty. For boys, this usually happens at around 12 years old. This is when the process of becoming an adult begins. (For more on puberty, see page 61).

4. By around 21 years old, a human will be a fully grown and developed adult. Adult life will now last until death, which can very rarely be predicted.

LIVING THINGS AND THEIR HABITATS

ANIMAL LIFECYCLE

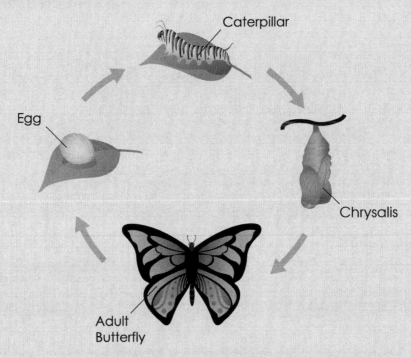

Of course, lifecycles across the animal kingdom vary hugely, depending on what species it belongs to.

As an example of a particularly unique animal lifecycle, let's look at that of a butterfly:

1. A female lays her eggs on a leaf so that what emerges does not have to go far to find food.

2. When ready, a caterpillar eats its way out of the egg – that's right, a caterpillar is actually a baby butterfly. It then starts to eat through as many leaves as possible.

3. Once it has eaten enough, the caterpillar is then able to form itself into a chrysalis (or pupa), a hard shell that protects itself from the outside world, where it begins to transform into a butterfly.

Question 1

Anil needs your help! He has a list of **vertebrate animals** that he has seen in the wild, which he wants to classify into groups. He is having trouble with this.

Look at his list of animals and their descriptions and decide whether it is a **mammal**, **amphibian**, **reptile**, **bird** or **fish**, writing your answer in the boxes below.

Anil's Animals

1. Common toad – females lay eggs in water, which develop into tadpoles and eventually new toads.

2. Red fox – body covered in fur, mothers produce milk to feed babies.

3. Bat – warm-blooded and furry, but capable of flight. Mothers give birth to live young.

4. Robin – red-breasted and feathery in appearance. Their chicks hatch from eggs in nests.

5. Grass snake – moves fast even though it has no legs. Scaly and cold-blooded.

6. Trout – seen in a local river, has gills and a scaly body.

ANIMAL 1	ANIMAL 2	ANIMAL 3	ANIMAL 4	ANIMAL 5	ANIMAL 6

Question 2

Look at the following pictures of **invertebrates** and answer the questions.

a)

Is the ant an insect or an arachnid?

_____

How can you tell? Give at least two reasons.

_____

_____

b)

Is the scorpion an insect or an arachnid?

_____

How can you tell? Give at least two reasons.

_____

_____

c)

How can you tell that the worm is not an insect or arachnid? Give at least two reasons.

_____

_____

d)

How can you tell that the jellyfish is not a mammal, amphibian, or even a fish? Give at least two reasons.

_____

_____

Question 3

Look at the pictures of the following plants and decide whether they are **flowering plants** or **non-flowering plants**.

a) Lavender bush

_____

b) Algae

_____

c) Mango tree

_____

d) Moss

_____

Question 4

Anil needs your help! He is writing a letter to a company that wants to build a factory on land where there is currently a forest, but he has left some gaps in his writing. He wants to let the company know that he disagrees with their decision to build there as it would badly affect the local wildlife.

Help Anil by filling in the gaps in his letter:

Dear Sir/Madam,

I am writing to let you know that the people of Verdant Valley are not happy with your decision to build a factory here. Cutting down trees will destroy the _____ of far too many animals, including insects, mammals and birds. This would mean that huge numbers of animals would die, because they would not be able to find _____ or _____ .

Humans have a great effect on the _____ around us, so it is our duty to make sure that it is protected and animals can survive. If one animal dies out, this can cause many others in its food chain to also _____ , and we can't let this happen.

Finally, a factory would releases harmful _____ into the atmosphere, which will harm everything from plants to humans.

Thank you for reading this letter, and please reconsider your plans.

Anil

Question 5

Match the stages of human life to their descriptions by drawing lines between the boxes. <u>The first one has been done as an example.</u>

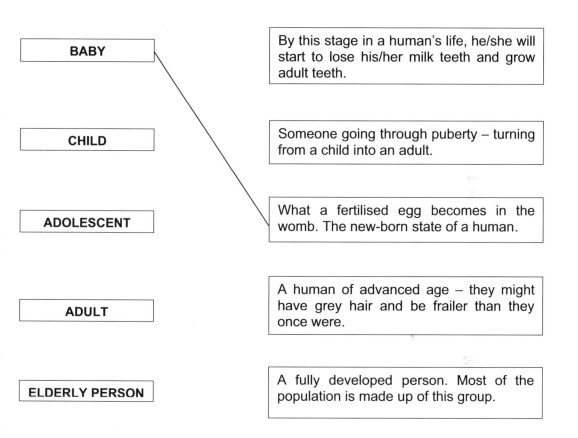

BABY

By this stage in a human's life, he/she will start to lose his/her milk teeth and grow adult teeth.

CHILD

Someone going through puberty – turning from a child into an adult.

ADOLESCENT

What a fertilised egg becomes in the womb. The new-born state of a human.

ADULT

A human of advanced age – they might have grey hair and be frailer than they once were.

ELDERLY PERSON

A fully developed person. Most of the population is made up of this group.

ANSWERS TO LIVING THINGS AND THEIR HABITATS

Question 1

ANIMAL 1	ANIMAL 2	ANIMAL 3	ANIMAL 4	ANIMAL 5	ANIMAL 6
Amphibian	Mammal	Mammal	Bird	Reptile	Fish

Question 2

a) The ant is an insect.

It has six legs and a body made up of three sections.

b) The scorpion is an arachnid.

It has eight legs and a body made up of two sections.

c) You can tell that the worm is neither an insect nor an arachnid as it has no legs or eyes, and is not made up of multiple sections – it has one long body.

d) You can tell that the jellyfish is not a mammal, amphibian or fish because it has no spine, it has no brain/heart and it has no gills.

Question 3

a) Flowering plant

b) Non-flowering plant

c) Flowering plant

d) Non-flowering plant

Question 4

Dear Sir/Madam,

I am writing to let you know that the people of Verdant Valley are not happy with your decision to build a factory here. Cutting down trees will destroy the **habitats** of far too many animals, including insects, mammals and birds. This would mean that huge numbers of animals would die, because they would not be able to find **food** or **shelter**.

Humans have a great effect on the **environment** around us, so it is our duty to make sure that it is protected and animals can survive. If one animal dies out, this can cause many others in its food chain to also **die out**, and we can't let this happen.

Finally, a factory would releases harmful **fumes** into the atmosphere, which will harm everything from plants to humans.

Thank you for reading this letter, and please reconsider your plans.

Anil

Question 5

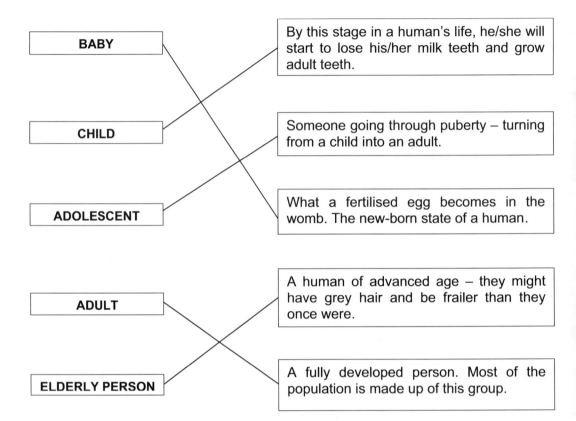

BABY		By this stage in a human's life, he/she will start to lose his/her milk teeth and grow adult teeth.
CHILD		Someone going through puberty – turning from a child into an adult.
ADOLESCENT		What a fertilised egg becomes in the womb. The new-born state of a human.
ADULT		A human of advanced age – they might have grey hair and be frailer than they once were.
ELDERLY PERSON		A fully developed person. Most of the population is made up of this group.

HOW ARE YOU GETTING ON?

THE
REVISION
SERIES

EVOLUTION AND INHERITANCE

EVOLUTION AND INHERITANCE

In this chapter, we will look at how living things on earth have changed over the millions of years that they have been alive, and the reasons for their changes. This will also involve looking at how certain animals and plants are specifically suited to their environment.

We will also look at how parents pass down characteristics and features to their offspring, and why children often have features that their parents do not have.

Superhero Freddie is going to show you three main things about evolution!

1. Evolution

2. Adapting

3. Inheritance and variation

EVOLUTION AND INHERITANCE

1. EVOLUTION

Evolution is the widely accepted theory to explain why life on earth looks and behaves the way it does, and both how and why species have very slowly, over millions of years, changed to increase their chances of survival in their particular environments.

How do the species change?

Through random genetic variation – this means that animals' offspring (children) are sometimes born with different physical features to their parents. (For more on variation, see section 3 of this chapter!)

Why do they change?

Sometimes, these random changes give the offspring an **advantage** in the animal's habitat. This means that the offspring with the features that give them this advantage are more likely to survive, and have offspring of their own.

So, the favourable feature is passed on again and again. Eventually, the only animals that survive in the habitat are those who possess this favourable feature, because those who do not have it are unable to compete. This is called **natural selection**.

One of the pioneering humans in observing this phenomenon was Charles Darwin (the man on the £10 note). He looked at birds on the Galapagos Islands, and noticed that each species of bird had evolved to have different shaped and sized beaks, which helped them eat the different kinds of food that appeared in the islands. This enabled the species to excel in their habitat.

Evolution in Action – Peacocks and Peahens

Male peafowl (peacocks) have evolved to have a hugely impressive plumage; they display huge and colourful feathers to attract a mate and have babies.

Imagine millions of years ago, there was a group of birds who had colourful feathers which they used to attract mates. Then, by chance, one bird hatched and grew larger and more colourful feathers than any other bird had before.

EVOLUTION AND INHERITANCE

When it reached adulthood, this bird was much more successful at finding a mate, so it was able to pass his impressive feathers on to the next generation. Eventually, this bird had several descendants, who were also very successful at finding mates. This meant that the birds with less impressive feathers could no longer find mates, because the competition had become too strong for them.

So, only birds with impressive feathers were being born, and the less colourful birds all died out. The species called peafowl (peacocks and peahens) was now firmly established, at the expense of the older, less successful species.

This was evolution and the idea of **survival of the fittest** in action.

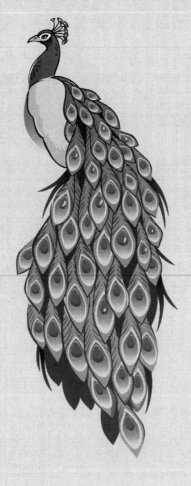

EVOLUTION AND INHERITANCE

2. ADAPTING

Now let's look at how certain animals have adapted to survive in their specific environment.

Red kangaroo:

The red kangaroo is only found in Australia, (due to the hot and dry conditions). As well as the adaptations listed below, they have also evolved to be able to survive on very little water and only eats grass, which has helped them survive.

Large ears

Hugely powerful legs

Long, muscular tail

Large feet

> **Large ears:** Its excellent hearing is one of the reasons that kangaroos have few natural predators. It can even swivel them around individually to help pick up sounds.

> **Large feet:** Provide an excellent base and springboard for their huge hop. Kangaroos have adapted to hop because it helps them move huge distances while using as little energy as possible: this is extremely helpful in the blistering Australian heat.

> **Hugely powerful legs:** The kangaroo's legs are extremely muscular to propel them forward with little effort.

> **Long, muscular tail:** This is used as a counterbalance, enabling the kangaroo to lean forward whilst hopping. This maximises momentum. A kangaroo's tail is also strong enough to be used to push off the ground for an extra speed boost.

EVOLUTION AND INHERITANCE

Polar bear:

The polar bear lives on and around the north pole of the earth, in countries including the Arctic, Canada and Greenland. So, it inhabits very cold climates full of ice and snow, feeding on nearly any type of smaller animal it can find; notably seals and reindeer.

Small ears

Large, strong legs

Thick, white fur

Large feet

➢ **Small ears:** Its small ears help the polar bear conserve heat – ears need to stick out to pick up sound, and if they were too big, the arctic wind would take too much heat from its body.

➢ **Thick, white fur:** The polar bear's fur allows it to survive in temperatures several degrees below freezing. It is also white so it can blend in with its surroundings and sneak up on unsuspecting prey.

➢ **Large, strong legs:** The polar bear's hugely powerful legs allow it to trek through thick snow for long periods of time, and attack and kill prey with ease.

➢ **Large feet:** Its large, rounded feet allows the polar bear to spread its weight across potentially thin ice, and pad across thick layers of snow without falling in.

EVOLUTION AND INHERITANCE

3. INHERITANCE AND VARIATION

Babies **inherit** features (like eye colour) from their parents. This is why that many children look similar to their parents.

However, most children are also born with features that their parents do not have.

This is called **variation**.

Variation exists so humans are not **identical** to each other. This is favourable for human survival; a variety of features means that we can survive in a variety of situations and climates.

As explored on the previous pages, variation makes evolution possible. Over millions of years, variation gradually makes animals more and more suited to their different habitats. Variation is the reason so many different species of animal exist!

Question 1

Below are four statements about animals and evolution, but three are incorrect. Put a tick (✔) in the box next to the one which is correct, and a cross (✖) in the three boxes to indicate the incorrect statements.

Animals realise that they need to develop helpful features to survive, so they evolve.

Animals have babies that have helpful features by chance, which help them survive. So, the helpful features are passed on.

Animals have always been as we see them today; 'natural selection' does not exist.

Not all species of animals, or plants, have had to evolve.

Question 2

Giraffes have evolved to have extremely long necks. How do you think that this helpful feature gave them an edge over competitors in the habitat, and helped them to survive?

_____

_____

_____

_____

Question 3

Below is a picture of a gazelle with arrows pointing to various parts of its body, all of which have developed to help it survive in its habitat and evade predators.

Label these using an adjective (describing word), to show how they are helpful features. One has been done as an example.

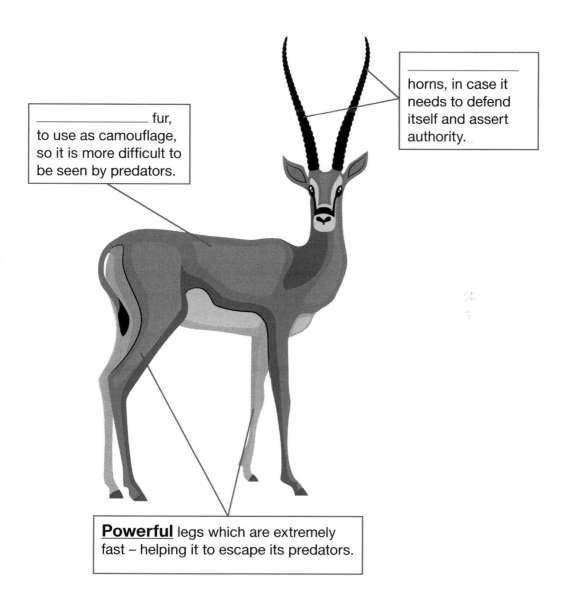

_____ fur, to use as camouflage, so it is more difficult to be seen by predators.

_____ horns, in case it needs to defend itself and assert authority.

Powerful legs which are extremely fast – helping it to escape its predators.

Question 4

Preston and Scarlett are having a conversation about variation and inheritance.

Preston says:

"Children are always born with the same hair colour as at least one of their parents."

Scarlett says:

"Children are sometimes born with completely different hair colour to that of their parents."

Who do you agree with, and why?

_____

_____

_____

_____

_____

ANSWERS TO EVOLUTION AND INHERITANCE

Question 1

Animals realise that they need to develop helpful features to survive, so they evolve.

Animals have babies that have helpful features by chance, which help them survive. So, the helpful features are passed on.

Animals have always been as we see them today; 'natural selection' does not exist.

Not all species of animals, or plants, have even had to evolve.

Question 2

Giraffes' long necks have helped them survive as they have allowed them to reach food in places that other species cannot. For example, giraffes can eat leaves straight from the branches of tall trees. This has made them a very successful species.

Also, giraffes' long necks also allow them to look for approaching predators.

Question 3

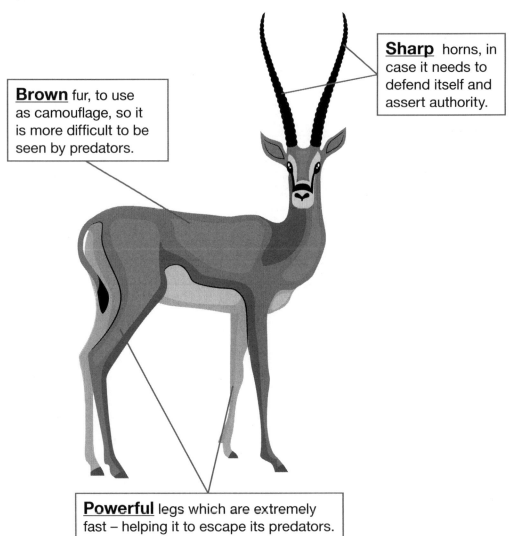

Brown fur, to use as camouflage, so it is more difficult to be seen by predators.

Sharp horns, in case it needs to defend itself and assert authority.

Powerful legs which are extremely fast – helping it to escape its predators.

Question 4

Scarlett is correct. Although it is common for a child to have the same colour hair as at least one of their parents, it is possible for a blonde child to be born to parents who both have brown hair. This is usually only possible if at least one of the parent's ancestors also had blonde hair.

WANT MORE SCIENCE PRACTICE QUESTIONS?

WHY NOT TAKE A LOOK AT OUR KS2 MATHS GUIDES!

FOR MORE INFORMATION ON OUR KEY STAGE 2 (KS2) GUIDES, PLEASE CHECK OUT THE FOLLOWING:

WWW.HOW2BECOME.COM